BANARAS

*

SARNATH

BANARAS
*
SARNATH

Lustre Press
Roli Books

The ghats along the riverside of Ganges, the holiest watercourse in India, seen in the early morning light. Some of the ancient ghats are many centuries old and some of them are known by the names of the donors (Scindia ghat, Bhonsale ghat) who helped build them. The ghats stretch for five kilometres along the winding riverfront.

AN.YOUTH.WELFARE.SOCIETY.
(भालू गुरु) (REGD)

The Ganges flowed in heaven. King
Bhagiratha appealed to Lord Brahma to let
the Ganges flow on earth and persuaded
Lord Shiva to catch it in his hair as it fell to
earth to prevent the planet from being
shattered by its torrential force. Here, the
wall painting depicts this story.

*G*anges or Ganga is the holiest river in India. It is the archetype of all the world's sanctified waters and is revered as both, goddess and mother. Its ritual purity negates everything inauspicious. A dip in the river purifies the sins of the living and ensures the salvation of the dead. It also symbolises shakti or the power of the feminine principle in life. Every day is a special day in Banaras with particular rites to be performed in observance of some festival or the other. As such, taking a dip or bathing in the holy waters of the Ganges at various places at various

times confers grace on the devotee. This is particularly so during the festivals. Likewise, early morning is seen as the best time for bathing in the holy water with the first rays of the sun breaking through the clouds in the east. When people bathe in the holy Ganges, they take up the water in their cupped hands and pour it into the river as an offering. A bath in the Ganges has sacred and cultural connotations that go back centuries. It is a cleanser of all sins. It is the protective mother from which all reality flows and to which everything returns for protection and purification.

After a bath in the sacred waters of the Ganga, cleansed of all impurity and sin, the devotee feels he or she is in union with the divine. The women bathe in the river and return to the steps of the ghats where they dry their saris in the strong riverside breeze. It is believed that even one drop of Ganga water can sanctify an entire river or ocean; it can purify and cleanse a person of all the sins of many lifetimes.

The Nandi bull is located outside, at the entrance to all Shiva temples. Here, this rare picture shows a Nandi bull inside the sacred precincts of a temple.

Sadhus *are holy men who have renounced the pleasures of this world. Some shave their heads bald or with a tuft at the back. Some grow their hair unshorn and wear it matted, as in this picture. Many of them are accomplished musicians or wrestlers. Quite a few of them smoke marijuana in* chillums *or clay pipes which are shown in the picture.*

Time Past in Time Present

*

KASHI, the luminous one, is the other name of Banaras. In this city of light, each dawn is a miracle. The sky lights up slowly, silently. As the first rays are shattered into gold on the waves of the quietly flowing river, the throng along its banks greets the universe and its creator. Waist deep in water, hundreds of Hindus face the rising sun and, as the dark river begins to glimmer, they cup the now golden water in their hands, raise it to the sun and then pour it back into the river, an offering to the gods, murmuring under their breath the great Gayatri Mantra:

Om Bhur Bhuvasva
Tat Savitur Varenium
Bhargo Devasya Dhimahi
Dhiyo Yo Nah Prachodayat
(Lord we behold your light that fills the three worlds, And pray for your radiance to illumine our minds.)

The Gayatri Mantra is a hymn from the *Rig Veda*—one of the four sacred Vedas of the Hindus, and the earliest known religious text in the world. The *Rig Veda* was composed some time between 1500-1000 BC by nomadic tribesmen called Aryans, living on the Indus plain in the region now known as Punjab. They began migrating southwards into the Indo-Gangetic plains from 1000 BC and, if the historians are right, the first man would have recited the Gayatri Mantra on the banks of the Ganges in Kashi some time between 800-900 BC. From then onwards, a period of about 3000 years, the same words and the same gesture have greeted the rising sun every morning at Banaras. Empires have risen and fallen, the bourgeoisie and the working class have replaced the priest and the aristocrat at the axes of power, amidst all these changes one thing has remained constant: the sun has risen every day in Banaras to its offerings of glittering drops of holy Ganges water. There are many things remarkable about this city, but nothing is more remarkable than the continuity of its religious and cultural traditions, even as it has grown and evolved over the years.

Even before the coming of the Aryans in 800-900 BC, the city of Banaras was alive and flourishing. Archaeologists digging at Raj Ghat, a plateau lying on the north-eastern outskirts of modern Banaras, have found evidence of a pre-Aryan settlement. Ancient

Facing page: Banaras or Kashi, to use the old name, is a timeless place. It is famous for its wrestlers who have their akaras (wrestling arenas) on the ghats. The picture shows two sadhus, a wrestler and a bull-calf; you cannot go very far in Banaras without bumping into one or all of them. They are there, everywhere.
***Above:** A holy man with his body smeared with auspicious vermilion.*

Sanskrit texts also bear this out. In the *Atharva Veda* dated 1100-900 BC, we find one of the Aryan priests requesting the malarial fever to leave his people and go to the people of Kashi instead. This suggests not merely that the people of Kashi, professing a non-Aryan faith, were viewed as the 'enemy', but also that Kashi was important and well-known even at that early date. The chosen city of the Hindus is in fact older than Hinduism itself.

Who were the earliest inhabitants of Banaras? What happened to them after the arrival of the Aryans? From literary sources of the period it is apparent that the Aryans defeated and established their suzerainty over the local inhabitants. With the fine contempt of the conqueror for the conquered, they classified the local inhabitants as *dasas* or slaves. Historians now suggest that these *dasas* were actually Dravidians—descendants of the survivors of Harappa and Mohenjodaro.

If that is so, then the so-called *dasas* were not an ordinary lot. Although inferior to the invaders militarily, they were definitely superior culturally. As the excavations of Harappa and Mohenjodaro show, the Dravidians had developed a sophisticated urban life-style based on agricultural surplus a full thousand years before the Aryans. They had also a full-fledged religion of their own, worshipping mother goddesses and a male deity called Pashupati, the Lord of the Beasts, who in many respects resembles Shiva, the Lord of Banaras now. They worshipped trees and animals, the chief being the *peepul* (*Ficus religiosa*) tree and the humped bull. In a sense, the victory of the Aryans over the Dravidians was a step backward for Indian civilisation; the Aryans were nomadic tribesmen when they arrived in the Indo-Gangetic plains, and it was only over a few centuries that they developed an urban culture and an organised religion of their own.

The establishment of Aryan suzerainty, however, did not mean the complete end of Dravidian culture and civilisation. It survived—but intermingled with the dominant Aryan beliefs and in course of time a synthesis of Aryan and non-Aryan practices did emerge, and it is this synthesis that in modern times is known as Hinduism. That Banaras was one of the major centres where this synthesis developed is obvious from the fact that to this day both Aryan and pre-Aryan forms of worship are most clearly visible here. Banaras thus marks the confluence not only of two rivers Varna and Assi after which it is named, but also of the two races whose descendants now inhabit the country.

With a recorded history of about 3,000 years and an unrecorded one going further back, Banaras is one of the oldest living cities of the world. Sherring, an Englishman, wrote in the mid-nineteenth century:

> Twenty-five centuries ago, at the least, it was famous. When Babylon was struggling with Nine-veh for supremacy, when Tyre was planting her colonies, when Athens was growing in strength, before Rome had become known or Greece had contended with Persia, or Cyrus had added lustre to the Persian monarchy, or Nebuchadnezzar had captured Jerusalem, and the inhabitants of Judaea had been carried into captivity, she had already risen to greatness, if not to glory.

In a very real sense modern Banaras is more than a city—it is a museum palpitating with life. Time past—and it is a long past—is contained in Time present, and one can trace in its gods and goddesses, in its temples, sacred ponds and wells, in its ghats and festivals, in its narrow lanes and crowds, in its pilgrims, ascetics, priests and philosophers, the very evolution of Indian civilisation.

Facing page: Behind the flower strewn statue of Shiva, in a niche in the wall of the Dashashivamedha ghat, the old man in saffron, who has come to Banaras for this very purpose, is waiting to die in the shelter of Shiva. People come to Banaras to die because it means salvation.

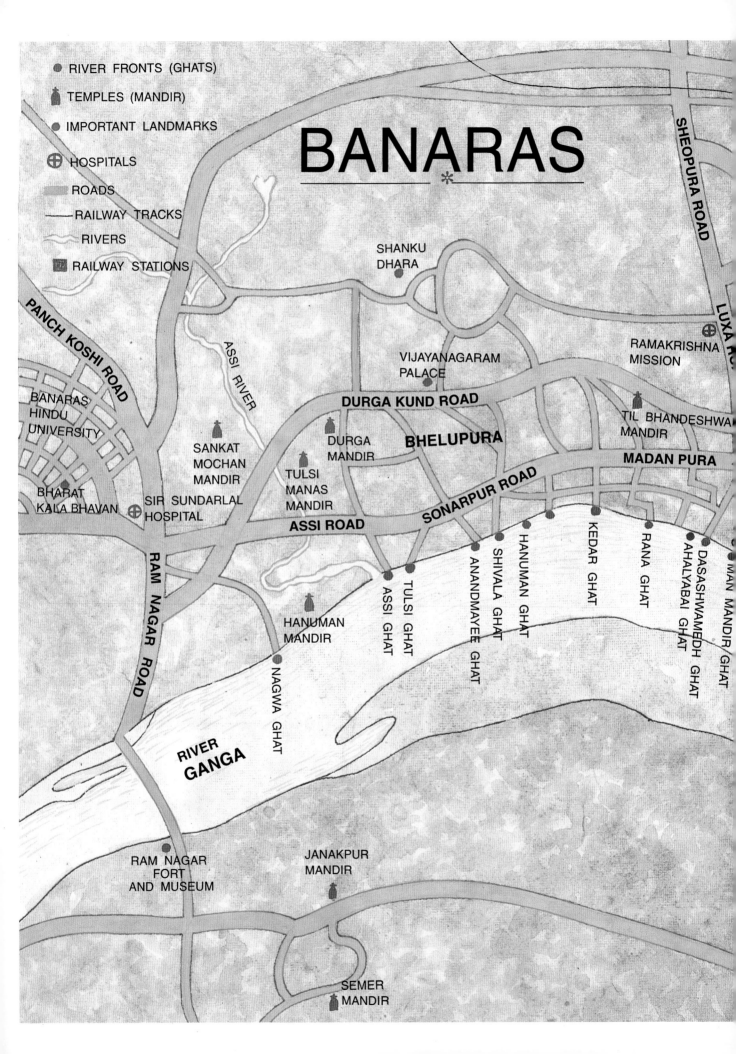

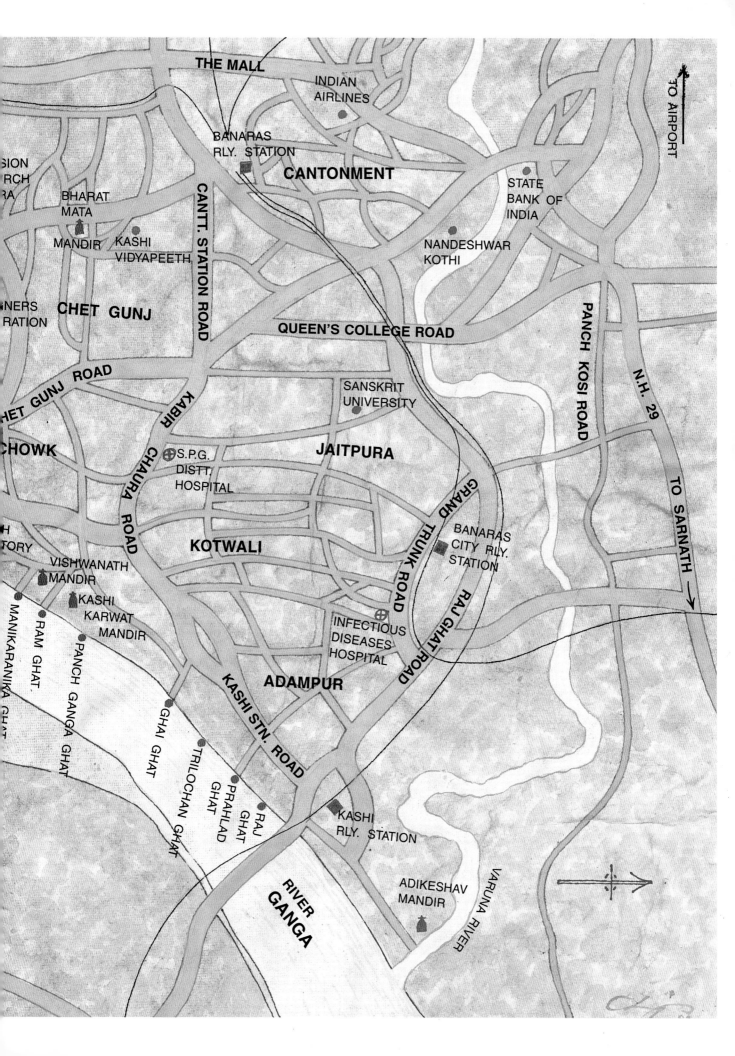

Sights and Insights

*

ONE HAS to scratch the surface of Banaras for commonplace sights and events to yield a wealth of meaning. The priest on the ghat, the wandering mendicant, the pilgrim at his devotions, the funeral processionists weaving through narrow lanes—everyday humdrum images can reveal themselves as fascinating composites of history and myth-making, of the mundane and the transcendental, of the real world and the imagined. Let us look around, then, and see what lies behind some of the most familiar sights in Banaras.

The Brahmin Pandas

You cannot miss them; they dominate the ghats. With bulging bellies, they sit on rectangular wooden benches under picturesque bamboo umbrellas, ministering to the needs of the pilgrims. They perform bathing rituals, apply *tilak* (the sandalwood mark on the forehead), guard the clothes of

Facing page: Sadhus *from all over India come to Banaras in various forms of transport. If a pilgrimage to Banaras is a must for every devout hindu, it is all the more so for the* sadhus *who congregate here in great numbers. Here,* sadhus *atop a caparisoned elephant lead a procession down a busy Banaras street.*
Above: *Devotees on a pilgrimage with one of them wearing a yellow shawl printed with the name of Lord Ram in red.*

their pilgrim patrons while they dip and pray in the Ganges and accept the *daan* or ritual gift for their services.

The *Pandas* are priests-cum-travel agents: they also meet the pilgrims at the railway station and make arrangements for their stay, either in their own houses or in rest houses. Sometimes the *Panda*-pilgrim relation continues over generations, with the descendant of a particular *Panda* family ministering to the descendants of a particular pilgrim family for hundreds of years.

The *Pandas* have a significant function to perform for the *Panchtirthi* pilgrims who flock to Kashi in thousands. The *Panchtirthi* pilgrims walk along the river front and have ritual baths at five of the holiest ghats—Assi, Dasashvamedha, Manikarnika, Panch Ganga and Raj Ghat. They also worship the prominent deities associated with these ghats. It is believed that the gods grant the pilgrim whatever he desires if he performs this particular pilgrimage. When starting the *Panchtirthi*, the *Panda* performs a ceremony stating the special purpose of the pilgrimage. Many pilgrims, of course, undertake it simply as an act of piety.

The *Pandas* are part of the larger Brahmin community of Banaras, which in turn is made up of *Pandits* (scholars), *Pujaris* (temple priests), *Mahants* (heads of temples and religious establishments) and

Vyasas (story-tellers). Banaras has traditionally been the stronghold of the Brahmins and it is they who have preserved ancient Sanskrit learning and the ritual traditions of Hinduism.

In later times rituals came to be practised because they were the only real identifying feature of Hinduism and were merely a means of intercession with the gods for worldly ends. In modern times rituals are performed on occasions of birth, death or marriage.

The Sanyasis

The Sanyasis, distinctive in their faded orange clothing, are people who have given up a settled domestic life and become perpetual wanderers and seekers. They usually have long, matted hair and carry a stout staff and a water pot. You can hear their cry in the streets of Banaras as they go from house to house asking for food: '*Ma, anna do.*' There are many kinds of Sanyasis. There are those

Previous pages 24-25 and above: *To bathe in the Ganges is to be cleansed of all sin.*

But the deteriorating economic condition of Brahmins who perform these rituals indicates their declining importance. The parasitism inherent in the Brahminic way of life often leads to corruption, and the *Pandas* of Banaras have earned a particularly bad name for themselves for cheating and robbing pilgrims.

If one is new to Banaras and its ways, it is safer to observe these gentlemen from a distance and understand what they represent, rather than have any dealings with them.

who have simply moved out of their homes into an ashram or *math* to study and meditate. Then there are those like the Aughurs, who not only renounce the world but turn its values upside down. They haunt cremation grounds, sleep on graves, eat food and drink water out of hollow human skulls and cook their food on cremation pyres. All the great orders of Sanyasis, the followers of Shankaracharya, Ramanujan, Vallabha and the tantric Gorakhnath have monasteries in Kashi where in the monsoon months, when travelling becomes difficult, they congregate from all over the country. After the monsoon, they are off again on their wanderings.

Why have these people renounced the world, and what is it that they seek? The answer to both these questions can be given in one word—*Moksha*. To understand this term and the lifestyle of the Sanyasis, one has to understand the essential mystical core of Hinduism. If the Brahmins are the

The Hindu term for this cosmic spirit is Brahma, and Brahma exists on two levels, the cosmic spirit that is outside us—that is, the permanent objective truth of the universe and on the other level, within us as *Atman*. *Atman* is our own inner subjective truth.

It is around the idea of Brahma and *Atman* that the entire edifice of Hindu philosophy is built.

The continuous passage of the *Atman* from body to body is often compared to a

During the festival of Kartik Purnima, which falls in October-November, lamps are lit in wicker baskets and raised on bamboo poles all along the river front, presenting a spectacular sight after sunset.

custodians of Hindu ritual, it is the Sanyasis who keep alive the metaphysical and mystical dimensions of Hinduism.

At the heart of Hinduism is a single vision—a profound consciousness of the wholeness of life, of the absolute indivisibility of the universe. It is, in fact, a vision of God in all things and all things in god. According to the Hindus there exists a cosmic spirit— infinite, deathless, creative and benevolent.

wheel in endless motion. In Hindu thought this process is considered to be infinitely tedious, and the desire for release from this endless cycle is universal. The term signifying this release is *Moksha*—considered to be the highest aim of existence. And that man with long, matted hair climbing down the steps of the ghats to the Ganges, staff in one hand and water pot in the other, might have already achieved it. At any rate,

if he is a true Sanyasi, he is working towards it.

Devotees and Pilgrims

You see them everywhere in Kashi—bathing in the Ganges, circumambulating the temples, paying homage to the gods with flowers, incense and sweets, and singing devotional hymns. They celebrate each of the Hindu festivals with great gusto and

to, not as an urban centre, but as a *dharma kshetra* (precinct of faith). The city is said to exist within a sacred concentric circle with a radius of five *krosha* (one *krosha* equals 9,000 yards), wherein all the sacred places of the Hindus are represented. The devotee here is supposed to undertake the five day *Panchkroshi* pilgrimage which involves a 50 kilometre trek circumambulating the entire city along the *Panchkroshi* road.

Wall-painting is a popular form of folk art in Banaras which is the city of Shiva, also called Avimukta, *the never-forsaken.*

flock in lakhs to the grand *melas* of Kashi. Such is their fervour and enthusiasm that often the entire city seems a vast arena of worship. In a way it is. In the ancient Sanskrit texts, Banaras is inevitably referred

Facing page: There are innumerable ashrams where the old folk who have renounced their earthly lives congregate to await their end in Banaras, ensuring salvation. The picture shows the entrance to one such ashram.

Kashi's importance as a religious centre lies in the fact that it is one of the greatest *tirthas* of the Hindus. The term *tirtha* means 'ford' or 'crossing place', and it refers to those places which are believed to be charged with power, where one crosses over from the material world to the world of spirit. There are thousands of *tirthas* all over India, but in the course of centuries the *Sapta Puri* (Seven Cities) and the *Char*

Dham (Four Great Abodes) have emerged as pre-eminent. The seven sacred cities are Ayodhya, in the north, where lord Rama ruled; Mathura, the birthplace of Krishna; Haridwar, where the Ganges descends to the plains; Kashi, the city of Shiva; Ujjain, in Central India, also sacred to Shiva; Dwaraka, the capital of Krishna, in the west, and Kanchi in the south, sacred to both Vishnu and Shiva. The Four Great Abodes mark the furthermost limits of the land—Badrinath in the north, Puri in the east, Rameshwaram in the south and Dwaraka in the west. Of all these sacred places Banaras is thought to be the holiest, for Banaras includes all the other *tirthas*, not just figuratively but literally. A visit to Banaras is considered equivalent to visiting all the other *tirthas* together, for it imparts to the pilgrims the merit of all the *tirthas* in a single pilgrimage. Naturally, pilgrims from all over the country flock to Banaras. The incessant activity of devotees and pilgrims in Banaras is rooted in a major development in Hinduism sometime around the first century AD—the introduction of idol worship. The early Aryans were not idol worshippers. Their dominant mode of relating to their gods was through ritual and sacrifice. Idol worship came to Hinduism through Mahayana Buddhism which by the first century AD had initiated the worship of the Buddha in the form of an idol. However, once introduced, the practice of idol worship transformed the religion completely.

Divinities were now conceived in human form and around these personalised gods, there slowly grew up the cult of *Bhakti* or devotionalism. The man who established the pre-eminence of the *Bhakti* cult among the Hindus was Ramanujan, an eleventh-century Dravidian scholar. Idol worship, in combination with Ramanujan's efforts shaped modern Hinduism and resulted in the Hindu pantheon of 330 million gods.

However, in course of time two gods, Vishnu and Shiva, emerged supreme, absorbing in themselves the other deities either as manifestations and incarnations, or as companions and consorts. In the north, Ayodhya and Mathura emerged as great centres of Vishnu worship, while Banaras remains, above all, the city of Lord Shiva.

Shiva's rise to pre-eminence is a fascinating illustration of the synthesis of Aryan and non-Aryan forms of worship. He was in all probability a non-Aryan god who was later incorporated into the Aryan fold, because he was too powerful or popular to be ignored. Among the great gods of the Hindus, Shiva is easily the god apart. He haunts cremation grounds, wraps snakes around his body, and has a terrifying retinue of followers called *ganas* and *bhairavas*.

Shiva defies all Aryan classifications because he does not belong to the Aryan order. He is not in the Vedas because he is older than the Vedas. By 1000 AD however, Shiva had been accepted as a god by the Aryans. With him came modes of non-Aryan worship: the non-Aryans practised fertility cults and worshipped female deities and the phallus. Shiva now is most commonly worshipped in the form of a *linga* (the phallic symbol). In Banaras a Shiva *linga* can be seen at every street corner, under every *peepul* tree. The Shiva *linga* consists of a cylindrical black stone set into a circular base. Some believe the linga to be more bisexual than phallic. They consider Shiva to be half man and half woman with the erect shaft of the *linga* representing the male aspect while the circular base female. There are many myths concerning the origin of the *linga*. But in the context of Kashi, the myth of the *Jyoti linga* —in which Shiva emerged from a *linga* of light—is more relevant as that was the first time the *linga* appeared in Kashi. Myths linking Shiva with Kashi are numerous. According to some, the city is located on ground created by Shiva on his trident. It is placed above the earth, such that the omnipresent law of Karma is not applicable here. In another popular myth Shiva is portrayed as a great ascetic who sits meditating atop the peak of Mount Kedar in the Himalayas. It is said that the energy which is generated by his meditation keeps the world functioning. It is this mountain ascetic that princess Parvati, daughter of the Himalayas, fell in love with and married. After scanning the entire universe for a suitable home for his bride and himself, Shiva chose the beautiful Kashi as his abode. He is said to have promised Parvati that he would never leave Kashi.

caused immense suffering. Brahma realised that there was only one man who could restore order and harmony, a philosopher-king in retirement in Banaras, named Divodasa. Brahma requested the king to rule over earth. Divodasa agreed but on the condition that all the gods should leave the earth and live in heaven. As a result Shiva, too, had to leave Kashi.

After some time, however, he began to pine for his beloved city. He first sent his

A priest on the ghat overseeing a ritual puja of ancestor worship when offerings are made to the departed.

That is why Kashi is also known as *Avimukteshwara*—the Never Forsaken.

Although Banaras is pre-eminently the city of Shiva, other Hindu gods are also represented and worshipped here. There is a popular myth that explains the presence of these other gods in Banaras. It is said that once there was a great drought on earth which destroyed the social order and

followers, the sixty-four female devotees called *yogins* and the *ganas* to Kashi, to try and lure Divodasa away. When these followers reached Kashi, they fell in love with the city. They not only failed to accomplish Shiva's mission, but abandoned it altogether and remained in Kashi. Shiva next sent the gods to find out what had happened to his followers and also to try

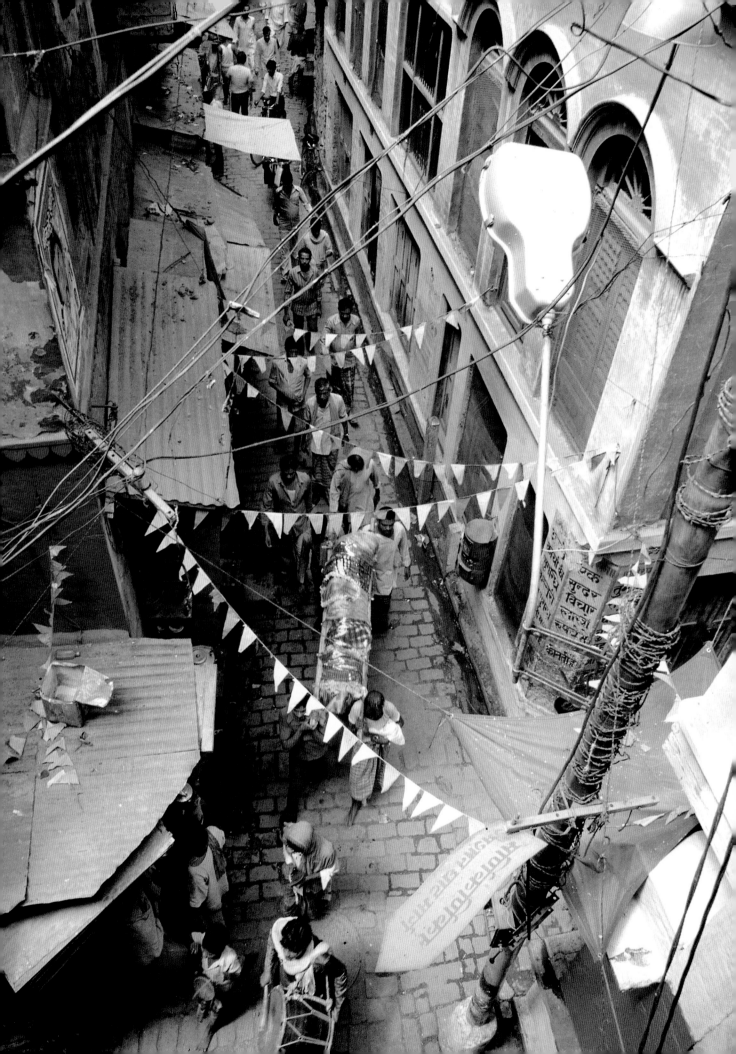

Funerals

*

YOU cannot move around Banaras for long without noticing the funeral processions. The dead body is carried on a stretcher decorated with flowers. At the head of the procession are seen relatives and friends of the deceased, moving to the accompaniment of a chant: '*Ram Nam Satya Hai* (Truth is God, God is Truth).' The procession terminates at the Manikarnika or Harishchandra Ghat, where the body is burnt on a pyre. Considering the number of funeral processions you are likely to encounter,

A corpse on a bamboo bier making its last journey through one of the narrow, twisting bylanes of Banaras.

you might justifiably wonder how, with so many people dying in it, Banaras is still so crowded. The answer lies in the special connotation the city has with respect to Karma and death. In the chosen city of Shiva, entry of Yamraj, the Hindu god of death is barred and every one who dies here is assured of *Moksha* and the concept of bad Karma and punishment in hell does not exist. It is said that at the moment of death Shiva reveals himself and whispers in the ears of the dying man the Taraka Mantra or the mantra of the 'Great Crossing', ensuring that he transcends the cycle of birth and death and becomes one with the universe. A mantra is a kind of formula which a guru gives to his disciple to open the doors of knowledge. Thousands of people from all over the country, therefore, come to Kashi to die and attain *Moksha*. Death holds no terror for one who dies in Kashi, for it is transformed by Shiva's blessing from a curse into one of life's most precious gifts.

Facing page: *Banaras is also known as* Mahasmashana, *the holiest cremation ground in all India. Dead bodies wrapped in silk brocades are carried on bamboo poles down the narrow bylanes to the burning ghats on their last journey.*

Previous pages 34-35, 36 and 37:
Manikarnika is the main cremation ghat in the centre of the ghats on the riverfront (Harishchandra ghat being the other). This is the most sacred site of liberation and salvation in all India. There is a well-attested belief that there is never a moment when a body is not burning on Manikarnika. By day, it is perpetually veiled in a haze of smoke from the burning corpses and by night the glow of fires can be seen from afar. To die in Banaras is to be liberated. Even people who die and are cremated elsewhere, send their ashes to Banaras for immersion in waters of the holy Ganges. It is the holy water of this river in this place that is offered by pilgrims and devotees in all acts of ancestor worship. The Doms are a caste of untouchables who are incharge of the cremation grounds where they sell wood and collect taxes for each corpse they burn. They are headed by the Dom Raja whose residence is depicted in the picture above, on this page. The Doms also have to tend the perpetual sacred fire from which all the pyres are lit.

and drive out Divodasa. But they too succumbed to the charms of the city. Shiva then sent Brahma, but he too fell under its spell. Finally, in desperation, Shiva sent Vishnu. Vishnu persuaded Divodasa to establish a Shiva *linga* in Kashi and make way for the god. Divodasa thus left for heaven, and Shiva returned to his beloved city with great joy, promising never to forsake it again. Ever since, the city is said to accommodate not

with every shrine. The great majority of temples honour Shiva in his various forms.

Vishwanath Temple: Varanasi is the city of Shiva, and this temple is the centre of Shiva worship in the city. Located in a crowded lane, neither big nor spacious, it is not a very impressive temple. But devotees throng to it in thousands to pray for worldly benefits and for *Moksha*.

It is difficult to say when this temple was first established, but it is probably as

The five-headed shiv-ling in the Tilbhandeshvar temple.

The gilded dome of the Vishwanath temple with the white minarets of a mosque in the background.

only Shiva but all the 330 million gods of the Hindu pantheon.

Temples

Banaras is a city of innumerable temples. There are legends and myths connected

Facing page: Ochre red is a much favoured colour used to smear idols and deities not only in Banaras but other parts of India.

old as Shiva worship in North India. It has had a chequered history, having been destroyed by Mughal rulers many times and yet rising, phoenix-like, again. The temple was destroyed for the last time by Aurangzeb in the seventeenth century and mosque was built in its place. Later the temple was rebuilt by the Marathas. The priests assert that the Shiva linga installed in the temple is the original one that has been

Previous pages 40-41: *A* Sadhu *of the Naga sect is depicted pouring a libation of holy water over the Shiv-ling. Banaras the luminous is Shiva's eternal city. As such, there are said to be billions of Shiv-lings in this city. Every nook and corner in every twisting bylane and* gali *will have Shiv-lings adorned with flowers and washed in holy water. The mythological belief is that Shiva appeared as an endless shaft of coherent light to end a dispute between Lord Vishnu and Lord Brahma, who with Lord Shiva, form the Hindu trinity. This is the generally accepted genesis of the Shiv-ling. The ling, a phallic symbol, is invariably set in a circular base expressing the feminine generative principle of* Shakti *or power. This is why Shiva is said to embody both the masculine and feminine principles.*

Above: *Inner precincts of a temple with a priest.*

Below: *Temple to goddess Durga popularly known as the monkey temple.*

Facing page: *Interior of temple near the cremation ghat of Manikarnika.*

worshipped for thousands of years. Apart from the Shiva linga there is also an image of Shiva, of which *darshan* is permitted only twice a year on special festival days.

The temple is located in the Vishwanath Gali. In and around the temple there are numerous other gods and goddesses, the most important being the goddess Annapurna, who shares the temple with Lord Shiva. Annapurna means 'provider of

The Nepali temple famous for its excellent carvings of Hindu gods and goddesses.

food', and in Varanasi the goddess is considered the mother who provides nourishment and sustains life. It is said that Shiva and Annapurna made a pact in Kashi: she would look after life before death, ensuring that no one every went hungry within the sacred city, while he would take care of life after death, ensuring that everyone from Kashi received *Moksha*.

The giving and receiving of alms is an important element of Hindu practice, and Annapurna is supposed to be the most generous alms-giver of them all. She sets an example which the citizens of Varanasi follow. By their alms the householders support the floating population of *sanyasis* and widows, who flock to the city. The temple itself does not serve as a charitable institution. It is just that the image of Annapurna as the generous mother sets an example for the householders to follow. There is a great festival called *Annakuta* which dramatises Annapurna's role as a provider of food. Mountains of food and sweets are elaborately arranged in the temple and later distributed as *prasad* to devotees who come to Annapurna on this day.

Kashi Karwat: The Kashi Karwat is another temple dedicated to Shiva. A deep, dry well located is the temple houses the reigning deity: a Shiva-*linga*. The story goes that an axe is placed next to the *linga* because people used to cut off their heads in a religious frenzy to attain *moksha*.

Tilbhandeshwar: The Tilbhandeshwar temple is yet another Shiva temple where the presiding deity is a *linga*. It is five feet high and growing every day by the size of a sesame (*til*) seed.

Durga: The Durga temple is a red, tiered edifice with trees on all sides. The place is crawling with monkeys. On special days, goats are sacrificed to goddess Durga.

Tulsi Manas: The Tulsi Manas is a temple of white marble which was built as recently as 1964. The temple is dedicated to Lord Ram and his consort Sita.

Bharat Mata: The Bharat Mata temple contains, in place of a deity, a graven map of India. The temple is open to people of all faiths.

Facing page: Interior of the Bharat Mata temple with a detailed relief map of (mother) India which is the sole deity here.

Above left: *Hanuman, the son of Vayu the wind-god is Lord Ram's chief ally and ideal devotee. Hanuman helped rescue Ram's wife Sita from Ravana by setting Lanka on fire. Hanuman is a very popular deity, specially in rural India.* **Right:** *Ganesh, the elephant-headed deity is the older son of Shiva and Parvati. He is universally invoked at the start of any new work, prayer or project as it is considered the most auspicious way to begin anything. He is often depicted with one broken tusk which he is believed to have used in writing the epic,* Mahabharata, *at the dictation of Vyasa. Most village plays and performances begin by propitiating Lord Ganesh.*
Below left: *Goddess Durga is the consort of Lord Shiva, but is worshipped and depicted in her own right as embodying* shakti *the feminine principle of power. She is shown as mild or fierce. Often she is depicted on a lion, with the decapitated head of Mahisasura, the demon. There are Kali (another name for Durga) temples all over India, the most famous one being in Calcutta.*
Facing page: *Monkeys abound in many temples. They are tolerated when they are not venerated. A monkey relaxes on a bronze statue of a lion.*

A Walk Down the Riverfront

*

ONCE UPON a time there was a king called Bhagirath whose ancestors had wilfully disturbed the deep meditations of a *muni* (sage) called Kapila. Kapila's angry glance burnt them to ashes and their souls were left trapped in the netherworld, unable to cross over to heaven. Bhagirath prayed to Brahma for advice to bring deliverance to his ancestors. Brahma told Bhagirath that their souls would be liberated only if their ashes were immersed in the cleansing waters of the river Ganges that flows in heaven. Bhagirath then prayed to the goddess Ganga to come down to earth. Though the ever-merciful Ganga agreed to help Bhagirath, there was a problem: if the river of heaven were to descend to earth directly, its force would destroy the world. Bhagirath solved the problem by enlisting Shiva's help. The god of the Himalayas received the shock of the torrent on his mighty head. Meandering through the forests of his locks, the river flowed out on to the earth, following

Bhagirath from the Himalayas to the point called Ganga Sagar in the Bay of Bengal, where it entered the netherworld and rescued the ancestors of Bhagirath. During this journey of the Ganges from the Himalayas to Ganga Sagar, trouble arose when it reached Banaras. Seeing the lovely city, Ganga did not wish to go further and almost turned back. It was with great difficulty that Bhagirath persuaded the river to carry on. If you look at the river in Banaras, you will see that it curves to the north almost as if flowing back in the direction of its source. And it is on this curve, shaped like a crescent moon, that the great stone ghats of Banaras have been built.

The Ganges is sacred everywhere in India, for the Hindus believe that the river washes away sin, and that if the ashes of the dead are immersed in it, the soul goes to heaven. But it is especially sacred in Banaras. The riverfront attracted in the past, and continues to attract today, not only millions of ordinary devotees but also some of the most famous men and women of India. The very gods, they say, come to bathe in the Ganges at Banaras. A walk down the riverfront is a walk down the flowing stream of Indian culture.

Facing page: Groups of ladies come early in the morning to perform ritual puja on the steps of the ghats.
Above: A devotee with his forehead marked with vermilion, kumkum, *sacred ash and sandalwood paste.*

Ghats

Assi Ghat: The southernmost ghat is known as the Assi Ghat, an assigned stop for both *Panchkroshi* and *Panchtirthi* pilgrims, named after the river Assi, which meets the Ganges at this point. On top of the ghat is an old Shiva *linga*, called Asisangameshwara. However, the focus of popular worship at this ghat is the Shiva *linga* located in the open, under a *peepul* tree. According to the Puranas (ancient Sanskrit texts), the goddess Durga threw down her sword at this spot, after killing the demon Shumbh-Nishumbh.

Tulsi Ghat: Next to the Assi Ghat is the Tulsi ghat, named after the sixteenth century author of *Ram Charitra Manas*. On top of the ghat is a temple of Ram and above it the house where Tulsi Das breathed his last.

Lolarka Kund: Above the Tulsi Ghat is the famous Lolarka Kund or pond with stone steps leading to it, which, some argue, is the most ancient sacred site of Kashi. Its presiding deity is the Sun, and its sacredness goes back to non-Aryan times when fertility cults were followed. Even now childless couples and those seeking a male child flock here in large numbers.

Shivala Ghat: The next important ghat is the Shivala Ghat. On top of it is the palace of Maharaja Chet Singh, who in 1781 fought against the British. People also believe that Kapil Muni, said to be the founder of the influential Sankhya school of philosophy, lived in this ghat sometime in the seventh century AD.

Hanuman Ghat: After the Shivala Ghat is the Hanuman Ghat, known for its Hanuman temple and as the place where the famous Bhakti saint Vallabhacharya lived and preached in the late fifteenth and early sixteenth century. The ghat has an image of one of the eight Bhairavas, manifestations of Shiva, who are supposed to assist Kal Bhairava in protecting the city from evil.

Harishchandra Ghat: Harishchandra Ghat is next. Also revered from ancient times, it is one of the two sacred burning ghats of Banaras, the other being Manikarnika Ghat. The ghat is named after a legendary king of Kashi, famous throughout the subcontinent for his virtue. Harishchandra was put to the test by the gods. Since the generous king was reputed never to have refused a request for alms, they sent a Brahmin named Vishvamitra to his court. Such were Vishvamitra's demands that the king could not satisfy him though he gave him all his kingdom. Eventually he surrendered his queen Tara and his son Rahul to work as domestic servants and sold himself into bondage to the *Doms* a social class who cremate dead bodies for a living, taking up their ghastly profession at the cremation ghat. The *Doms* assigned Harishchandra the task of collecting the ritual fee before allowing anyone to burn their dead. One day a poor woman came to the ghat with the body of her dead child; Harishchandra recognised her as his beloved wife and the dead child as his only son. Tara did not have the money to pay the ritual fee. Harishchandra knew that it was his responsibility as a father to provide the money for the last rites, without which the soul of the dead could find no peace. But he was a slave and had no money of his own. As the custodian of the burning ghat he could have allowed the cremation of his son for no payment. But Harishchandra was incapable of dishonesty, and the body was left exposed to the elements. It was then

Facing page: Above Tulsi ghat, at the Lolarka Kund, women gather to celebrate Lolarka Shashthi. They bathe and worship the sun god by offering him gourds and other vegetables.
Pages 52-53 overleaf: Women drying their saris in the sun after a dip in the Ganges. The temple in the background is regularly submerged under water when the river-level rises.

that the gods admitted defeat, realising that nothing in the world could tempt Harishchandra. His son was restored to life and his kingdom returned to him.

Kedar Ghat: The next important ghat is the Kedar Ghat, named after the Kedareshwara temple built on the ghat. Close to the ghat is also the Gauri Kund. Both the *kund* and the temple are widely known in the city. The temple, very popular among the Bengalis who live

Nag Panchami in July or August, perhaps the most important in the worship of snake deities, people gather here in thousands to honour them.

Ahalyabai Ghat: Next comes the Ahalyabai Ghat built by the Maratha queen Ahalyabai.

Dasashvamedha Ghat: Ahalyabai Ghat is followed by the most popular ghat of Banaras today, the Dasashvamedha Ghat. The name means 'the sacrifice of ten

The devotee seated in the centre is performing jap *the ritual repetition of a mantra or the holy name of god.*

around the ghat, contains images of Ganesh, Laxmi and Annapurna who are prominent in the Hindu pantheon of gods.

Chauki Ghat: Chauki Ghat, which follows Kedar Ghat, is known for the huge tree that stands on top of the steps. Under the tree there are a number of stone *nagas* or divine snakes. On the festival of

horses', apparently performed here by the legendary king Divodasa. The southern part of the ghat is known as Rudrasara or Rudrasarovar. The most prominent temple here is that of the goddess Shitala, who is supposed to cure people of smallpox and measles.

Prayag Ghat: The northern part of the ghat is called Prayag Ghat, named after the famous *tirtha* further down the river. The Dasashvamedha Ghat houses three ancient Shiva *lingas*—the Brahmeshwara, the Shulankeshwara and Dashvamedeshwara. The famous Vishwanath temple is easily reached from this ghat.

Man Mandir Ghat: After Dasashvamedha Ghat comes Man Mandir Ghat, built by Man Singh, the commander-in-chief of the great Mughal emperor Akbar. One of the attractions of this ghat

in the early eighteenth century. But Mir Ali took to the Banarasi way of life with such aplomb that, though he was a Muslim, songs about him are sung to this day by the Hindu citizens of Banaras. Fond of music and dance, Mir Ali is said to have started the famous festival of Budhwa Mangali. The festival, probably the only one of its kind in the world, was for long the high point of life in Kashi. But after 1940, Budhwa Mangali festivities began to

Shiv-ling puja in the early morning sunlight.

is the observatory built by the Rajput king, Raja Jai Singh of Amber, in the eighteenth century. On the ghat is located an old Puranic *linga* called Someshwara.

Mir Ghat: Next comes Mir Ghat, named after one of the most colourful personalities ever to have lived in this city. Mir Rustam Ali was appointed the Governor of Kashi by the Nawab of Avadh

degenerate into an orgy and were thus stopped.

Lalita Ghat: Lalita Ghat, which comes after Mir Ghat, was built by the King of Nepal and is named after his mother. On top of the ghat is a beautiful temple of Mahadeva Pashupatinath made out of wood and carved in the beautiful Nepali style.

Above: *Offering holy Ganga-water to the gods at first light of day. Women take the holy water of the river in their cupped hands or a vessel and pour it back into the Ganges as a libation. It is at once, an offering to Goddess Ganga, all the gods and one's departed ancestors.*

Below: *Aarti, ritual offering on a plate with fire, rice, camphor and other articles used in daily worship. The ritual offering of* aarti *is being done by a priest to the chanting of prayers accompanied by drums and cymbals. Garlands of marigold flowers are used in worship.*

Facing page: *Festival of Dalachchat where devotees take a dip in the sacred waters before making offerings to the river goddess, Ganga. Devout crowds mob the waterfront in a holy frenzy of piety.*

Manikarnika Ghat: Next is Manikarnika Ghat, by far the most sacred of the holy ghats of Banaras. It is said that the sanctity of Manikarnika pre-dates the coming of the Ganges to Banaras. According to myth, this is the place from which Shiva created the universe, and it is this spot that will survive when the entire universe is destroyed. Located at the centre of the ghat is the Chakrapushpani Kund, said to have been Hindu there can be no place holier than this. A dip in the river at this ghat is a must for all pilgrims and devotees in the city, and thousands bathe here every day.

Manikarnika Ghat is also the most sacred cremation spot of Banaras. Hindus believe that anyone cremated here achieves *Moksha*. The most important Shiva *linga* on the ghat is the Tarakeshwara, whose presence at Manikarnika is appropriate because it is here that Shiva allegedly

After the cremation, the male relations of the deceased are tonsured as a mark of mourning.

carved out by Vishnu and filled with his own perspiration. It is in this pool that Goddess Parvati is supposed to have dropped her earrings (*mani*, jewel, and *karnika*, earrings) while bathing. On the steps, a few yards from the water, are the footsteps of Vishnu set in a marble slab. The spot is sanctified by Shiva, Vishnu and the Ganges and for the whispers the Taraka Mantra into the ears of the dying to ensure that they attain *Moksha*. There is also the goddess of Manikarnika here, who is worshipped locally. The great Vishwanath temple is easily accessible from this ghat, and a dip in the Ganges here is usually followed by a visit or *darshan* at the temple.

Panch Ganga Ghat: If Dasashvamedha

is the most popular ghat and Manikarnika the holiest, then Panch Ganga is surely the most impressive. It is also one of the five major ghats where the *Panchtirthi* pilgrim must bathe. This ghat is dominated by a mosque built by Aurangzeb. Earlier, the mosque was a temple dedicated to Vishnu known as Vindu Madhav, but in the sixteenth century, Aurangzeb, the last of the great Mughals, had it destroyed and built the mosque in its place. It was on

Other Ghats: After the Panch Ganga Ghat come Brahma Ghat, Durga Ghat, Gaya Ghat and Trilochana Ghat. After Trilochana, most of the ghats are clay-banked. Beyond Raj Ghat is the Raj Ghat plateau. In ancient times the city of Banaras was located on this plateau and excavations here have yielded a lot of material which throws light on the 3,000-year old history of the city. On top of the ghat is the Adi Keshav or the temple

Wrestling is a favourite pastime in Banaras. Many akaras *or wreasting arenas, dot the ghats along the riverfront.*

this ghat that the great sage Ramanand finally accepted the *Bhakti* poet Kabir as his disciple. The ghat has been given the name Panch Ganga or the five Ganges, because it is said that four underground rivers—the Kiran, the Dhootpapa, the Dharmanand and the Saraswati—meet the Ganges at this point.

of the Original Vishnu, where Vishnu is said to have first visited when he arrived in Kashi to oust Divodasa on behalf of Shiva.

Pages 60-61 overleaf: *The banks of the Ganges overflowing with pilgrims. The river is associated with all festivals in Banaras.*

Festival of Life in the Lanes
——————— ✳ ———————

JUST BEYOND the ghats of Banaras is an incredible world of labyrinthine lanes that constitutes the heart of this ancient city. The Banarasi term for these interconnecting lanes is *gali* which can be defined as a narrow twisting track, one to four metres wide. They stretch from the Assi Ghat to the Raj Ghat in the dense habitation known as the *pucca mahal*. In earlier days it was this network of lanes that constituted the city of Banaras, for the main roads that connect Raj Ghat, Maidagin, Chowk and Gadowlia, were built only in the British era. These lanes are so narrow and dense that the sun's rays cannot penetrate to them. The only possible mode of transport is one's own feet, and these too must turn back if, as often happens, one faces a bull approaching from the other side. The bull is supposed to be the mount of Lord Shiva and, in this city where he rules, it is considered sacred. A long time ago a British administrator tried to rid the *galis* of the menace of these creatures, but had to give up the idea in the face of massive public opposition. Over the years the bulls have multiplied and now these large, rather ferocious creatures reign supreme in the narrow lanes of Banaras.

Facing page: A narrow, winding gali *in Banaras with a small shop selling articles of daily use.*
Above: Study of a priest on the ghats.

When two of them lock horns, as they often do, all hell breaks loose. Men, women and children fling themselves into safe corners or rush out of the combat zone as the two antagonists push and shove each other, sometimes right into the shops lining these lanes.

The narrowness of these *galis* has successfully kept modernity at bay and gone a long way towards creating and preserving the distinctive identity of the city. The lanes of Banaras present India in a crowded microcosm. People from all parts of the subcontinent have come and settled in these lanes. Those from Bengal live in Bengali Tola; those from Tamil Nadu and Karnataka live in the lanes at the back of Hanuman Ghat; the Punjabis live in Lahori Tola; the Gujaratis live in Suth Tola and Chaukhamba; the Nepalis live in Doodh Vinayak; the Maharashtrians live in Durga Ghat and Brahma Ghat; the Marwaris inhabit the lanes stretching from Mandan Sahu to Ram Ghat; the Sindhis have their colony near Soniya. The Muslims live in Madan Pura and Revadi Talab, and the Afghanis live in and around Deniya Bagh.

The infinite variety of everyday human life, with its essential concerns of health and sickness, work and recreation, its intellectual preoccupation with philosophy, music and poetry, its commercial pre-occupation with

buying and selling and its emotional pre-occupation with sympathies and antipathies is to be seen at its richest within these lanes.

For centuries now the *galis* have been alive with the sound of music. Go anywhere into the lanes behind Iswar Gangi, or into the lanes stretching from Dufferin Hospital to Nagri Natak Mandali, and you will hear the sound of musical instruments like the *tabla* or the *sarangi*, or the strains of

as the city itself. However, the beginnings of the classical tradition of Indian music for which the city is famous can now be dated to the sixteenth century. The courtesans of Banaras have played a significant part in the development of this tradition.

Names like Pandit Ravi Shankar (*sitar*), Ustad Bishmillah Khan (*shehnai*), Shambhu Nath Mishra and Sumernath (*sarangi*), the *gharanas* or schools of Pandit Ram Sahay and Pandit Biru Mishra (*tabla*), have

Kishan Maharaj, the great tabla *(percussion instrument) player of Banaras, paying obeisance to Lord Ganesh.*

someone practising vocal music. There are perhaps more musicians in Banaras than in any other city of the country. Of course no systematic account of the development of the tradition of music in Banaras exists, for the simple reason that the tradition is as old

Facing page: *Music is an integral part of daily life in Banaras which has produced great musicians like Ustad Bismillah Khan, Girja Devi, etc. The picture shows a skilled technician making a* sitar.

become legendary. Banaras has also produced dancers like Gopi Krishna and vocalists like Prasidh, Manohar, Jagdeepji and Majnuddin Khan. The list of names goes on. Nowhere else in India has music been studied and performed with greater skill and in greater variety.

With all their cultural wealth, the primary importance of the *galis* remains economic: the entire commercial activity of the city is conducted within these lanes. Banaras was widely known as a great trading centre in ancient times, the river Ganges providing an easy means of transportation. Excavations evidence that Banaras conducted a lively trade with Ujjain and Ghandhar. Banaras possibly traded with the Roman world, too, because there are old Roman references to a high quality muslin which was, in all probability, the famous *kasikavastra* produced in Banaras. The merchants trading on these routes were called *shresthis* and according to the *Jataka* tales (a collection of 550 stories of the former lives of the Buddha), which give a vivid picture of the economic activity of Banaras in ancient times, they used to amass vast fortunes.

What were these goods that were in demand the world over? To begin with there were textiles—cotton, wool and silk. In the ancient world, cloth from Banaras called *kasikuttam*, *kaseyka* or simply *kasiya* was famous the world over for its fine texture and softness. The cloth in which Buddha's body was wrapped after his death came from Banaras and was said to have been woven so fine that it could not absorb even oil. It was this splendid silk cloth embellished with gold thread and precious stones, which kings demanded for royal attire and to adorn their palaces.

The proud heritage of excellence of Banarasi fabrics is evident in the saris, whose distinguishing feature is its *zari* work—gold and silver threads woven into patterns. In earlier days the threads were made of real gold and silver. Now however, synthetic gold threads have taken their place.

Most of the other traditional handicrafts continue to flourish. Banaras is still famous for its gold and silver jewelry. Articles of domestic use, utensils, decorative pieces and ornaments, toys and figures made out of wood, metal and clay are still manufactured and sold. New handicrafts like carpet-weaving have also taken root in Banaras.

Vishwanath Gali

Easily the most famous lane in Banaras, it is located slightly to the east of the road that connects Raj Ghat to Assi Ghat. From north to south it is about 500 metres long. It starts at Devdasi-ka-pul and merging with the lanes of Bans Fatak and continues till the Annapurna and Kashi Vishwanath temples. Buildings three to four storeys high line the lane on both sides, effectively shutting out the sunlight. The *gali* is full of temples, *maths*, *dharamshalas* (rest-houses for pilgrims), *lingas* and images. Most of the shops occupy the outer sections of temples or religious institutions and they are so small and narrow that no customer can step inside.

Since the famous Vishwanath temple is located in this lane, a large number of shops sell objects of ritual and worship. However, other goods like utensils, toys, ornaments, jewelry, and toilet articles are also sold and sales transactions became a rigorous test of the business skills of both the shopkeeper and the customer. Most of the big shopkeepers pay a commission to guides to lure unwary travellers to their shops.

The religious, cultural and economic life of Banaras merge in this *gali* as nowhere else. It comes alive well before sunrise. Devotees, chanting 'Har, Har Mahadev!' or 'Shiva, Shiva !' go to the ghats for their ritual morning bath and then come back for a *darshan* at the Vishwanath temple. By 10 a.m. the crowd of devotees begins to diminish and the *gali* takes on a different aspect: shopkeepers and office-goers heading for their place of work, students on their way to schools and colleges. Shops open by about 11 a.m., but real business starts only in the evening. From 3 p.m. onwards the preoccupation of the *gali* is strictly secular. Sales are brisk, most of the customers being women. Later in the evening, everyone in the city seems to move towards the Vishwanath Gali—writers, students, poets, government servants, politicians, all congregate here, and *paan* (a heady betel leaf preparation) shops and tea stalls come into their own. This crowd disperses over the evening, and by 10 p.m. only those interested in witnessing the *aarti* (an essential ritual in Hindu worship) at the Vishwanath temple remain.

Economic prosperity down the ages has enabled the citizens of Banaras to devote considerable energy towards perfecting the art of living. Over the years a distinctively

the fullest. His is an ease born of the conviction that Shiva is in heaven and that heaven is none other than his own city. His is an open laughter, and his conversation does not suffer from the craven scruple of dwelling too precisely over the event.

It is the simple pleasures of life that give the Banarasi his elan. A bath in the river, a visit to the temple, a get-together with friends, dance, music and *mithai* (sweets), *thandai* (frozen almond milk) laced with

The Maharaja of Banaras in full ceremonial splendour on his way to witness the public staging of the Ram Lila.

Banarasi way of life has evolved with stress on values like *masti* and *mauj*, terms signifying a carefree, casual, joyous acceptance of life, so much so that a true Banarasi carries the stamp of his city wherever he goes. The Banarasi state of being is opposed to feelings of cynicism, depression and neurosis; a true Banarasi lives in the present, untroubled by the past, unworried about the future, enjoying life to

intoxicative *bhang* and—above all—*paan*.

Indeed, if there is one thing that symbolises the Banarasi's addiction to the good things of life, it is *paan*, made of betel leaf, *supari* (betel nut), *chuna* (lime) and, for those who want it, tobacco. The *paan* gives a mild high and is eaten all over India. According to one Banarasi writer, the joy of eating *paan* is indicative of the joy of *Moksha*.

Above: *A shop selling silk saris. Banaras is famous for its silk brocade. No wedding trousseau of a well-to-do bride can be considered complete without the inclusion of Banarasi sari(s). In the old days, Banaras silk saris were worked with real gold and silver threads that made these brocades priced possessions world-wide. Nowadays artificial yarns are used and yet the overall effect is aesthetically stunning.*

Below: *A portable* paan *shop on the ghats. One of the good things of life, Paan is chewed at all times of the day. It is supposed to be a digestive. Some take it with tobacco. It gives a mild high. The Banarasis specialise in the making of* paan *which is considered an art in itself involving as it does an etiquette of certain graces and gestures.*

Facing page: *A shop selling various articles involved in ritual worship. The piles of coloured powder are vermilion and* kumkum *in three shades of red, bead-rosaries used as an aid to the repetitive telling of mantras and prayers; containers to hold the holy Ganges water.*

Sadhus

S AGES, *sadhus* and *sanyasis* are people who having renounced the world and its earthly pleasures, spend their days and nights in meditation and prayer. Holy places of pilgrimage like Banaras are largely defined by these holy men who congregate there. They are said to believe that the constant repetition of the name of a god or a powerful phrase (*mantra*) can be internalised and

An Aghori Baba, his body smeared with ashes from the pyres of the dead, in the sirshasana *yogic posture.* **Facing page:** *A Naga* Sanyasi *standing naked amidst other* sadhus *in a crowded boat.*

synchronised with one's breathing, so that the utterance of the prayer lasts until death. They move from one place of pilgrimage to the other or from one major festival in a place to another somewhere else. Those not on the move, remain in one place, lost in prayer and meditation. Some give solace and advice to lay people seeking help in spiritual matters. Some practice harsh austerities like standing on one leg for so long that the muscles in the other leg wither away. Even birds are said to have built their nests in the hair of meditating hermits lost in fixity and prayer.

This and facing pages: *There are various sects of* sadhus, *each of whose practice differs from the others. But in one thing they are all united: the longing for union with the divine. The pictures show the varied faces of* sadhus *from all parts of the country; they take in all ages. The way they wear their hair and headgear is as different as is their apparel. The caste marks on their foreheads differ from person to person. But all these differences are as nothing when it comes to the manner in which they address themselves to the divine. Though the forms of God are many, they are merely viewed as aids through*

which to approach the supreme
being. The fallout of this inclusive
approach to religion lends colour
and diversity to the sadhus
themselves.

Pages 74-75 overleaf: *A group
of* sanyasis *relaxing round a fire
while in the background, a man
is making rotis, the flat
unleavened bread that is the basic
of the north Indian diet. In
Banaras, death is liberation from
the otherwise unending chain of
birth and rebirth. Even to sleep in
Banaras is said to be more potent
than doing yoga elsewhere.
Renouncers or* sadhus *from all
over India are drawn to Banaras.*

Living Landmarks

*

SANSKRIT **Vishvavidyalaya:** The Sanskrit Vishvavidyalaya is a full-fledged Sanskrit university, the only one of its kind in the country. About 500 students study traditional subjects like the Vedas, Sanskrit grammar and literature, Buddhist and Jain philosophy, Yoga and astrology. It is thus befitting that this unique university be located in Banaras

the next fifteen years, the student lived with the Guru who clothed, fed and educated him and during those years he took the vow of *brahmacharya* or celibacy. He could leave the Guru's house once his education was over and the mutually agreed upon remuneration paid to the Guru.

As a result of this practice in ancient

The Sanpoornanand Sanskrit Vishvavidyalaya is the oldest sanskrit university established in 1791.

which has been a great centre of Sanskrit learning for centuries.

In earlier days, education used to revolve around Brahmin households, for it was the duty of the Brahmins not just to perform religious ceremonies but also to impart Vedic learning to children of upper-caste Hindus. The system of education was simple: the student left home at the age of ten or eleven to live with a teacher who was known as the Guru or *Acharya*. For

India, the places where Brahmins settled in large numbers usually turned into great educational centres as well. Banaras, which had been a Brahmin stronghold from seventh century BC, was therefore also a great seat of learning to which students came from all parts of the country. During the Buddhist period, such was its renown that the *Jataka* tales refer to it as *Brahmavardhana*—the philosophical fountainhead.

In 1791, Jonathan Duncan, an agent of

the East India Company at Banaras, suggested to the Earl of Cornwallis, the then Governor-General, that,

> a certain portion of the surplus revenue of the province or *zamindari* of Benaras, should be set apart for the support of a Hindu college, or academy, for the preservation and cultivation of Sanskrit literature and religion of that nation, at this, the centre of their faith and the common resort of their tribes.

Banarasi nationalist leader Pandit Madan Mohan Malaviya in the early twentieth century became obsessed with the idea of combining the best elements of the Indian and Western intellectual traditions. He presented his proposal before the Indian National Congress in 1905 and won able and influential supporters in Dr Annie Besant and the Maharaja of Darbhanga in Bihar. He eventually collected enough funds from both the rich and the poor. The then

The palace of Kashi Naresh, the Maharaja of Banaras on the other side of the river facing the ghats. There is a special gate through which he emerges each morning to take a dip in the Ganges.

The result was the setting up on 28 October 1791 of a modest Sanskrit *pathshala* (school) in a rented house near Maidagin Tank. Later, this centre became the Government Sanskrit College and in 1958 it was elevated to the status of a university. The university continues the centuries-old tradition of Sanskrit learning, but obviously does not follow the traditional method of teaching.

Banaras Hindu University: The

Maharaja of Banaras, Prabhu Narain Singh, donated 1,300 acres of land and on 1 October 1917 a grand conception became a functioning reality. Malaviya became the Vice-chancellor of the university, in which position he continued till his death in 1946. At present the university is one of the largest in Asia, and it epitomises the love of learning that has been an ever-present reality in Banaras.

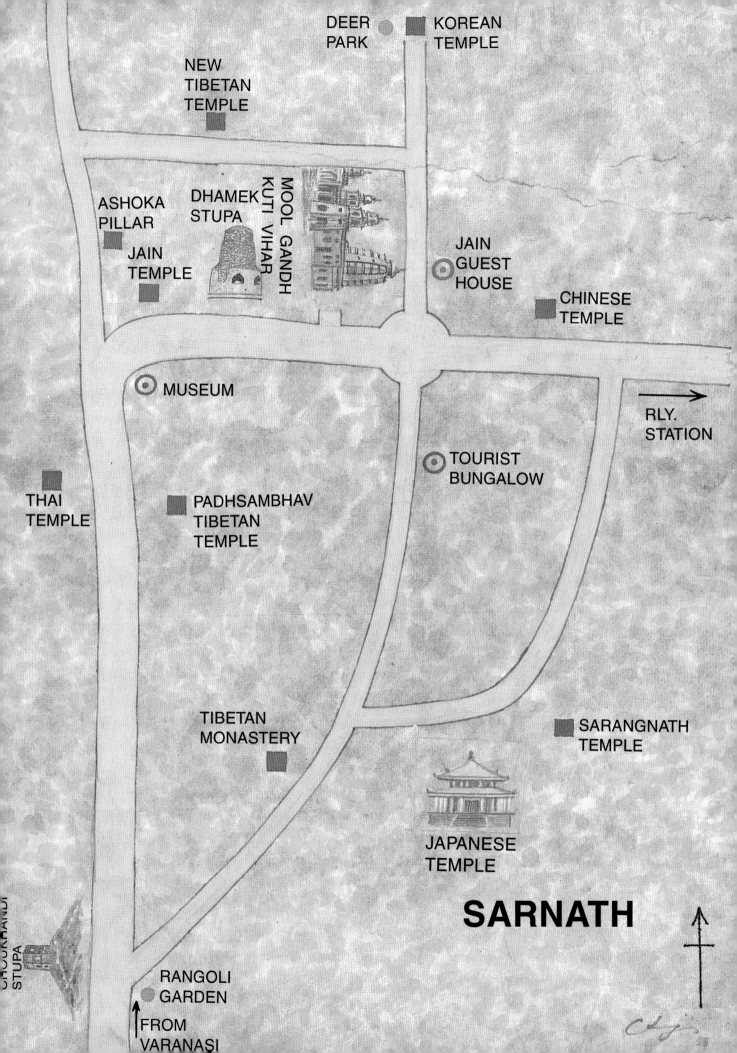

DEER PARK

KOREAN TEMPLE

NEW TIBETAN TEMPLE

ASHOKA PILLAR

JAIN TEMPLE

DHAMEK STUPA

MOOL GANDH KUTI VIHAR

JAIN GUEST HOUSE

CHINESE TEMPLE

MUSEUM

RLY. STATION

TOURIST BUNGALOW

THAI TEMPLE

PADHSAMBHAV TIBETAN TEMPLE

TIBETAN MONASTERY

SARANGNATH TEMPLE

JAPANESE TEMPLE

SARNATH

CHOUKHANDI STUPA

RANGOLI GARDEN

FROM VARANASI

Sarnath

— ✳ —

SARNATH, is one of the most important places of worship for Buddhists, the world over. Sarnath, about seven miles to the north of Varanasi, is a tiny hamlet where the

A Buddhist monk meditating.

Buddha preached his first sermon 2,500 years ago. Called 'The Turning of the Wheel' (*dharma chakra pravartana*) the sermon summed up the essentials of Buddhist teaching. Focusing upon suffering, the Buddha argued that the cause of suffering was desire, and that if man wished

to get rid of suffering he must first get rid of desire.

A wandering teacher during much of his life, the Buddha travelled over the eastern Gangetic plain, preaching his doctrines, but he often stayed at the monastery in Sarnath during the monsoon months. In later years, Sarnath became not only an important centre of Buddhist art and thought but also one of the holiest shrines of Buddhism, visited by devotees from all parts of the world.

it a place of suffering. Man's salvation lies in freeing himself from desire and achieving *nirvana* or extinction, freedom from the wheel of rebirth.

After the death of its founder, Buddhism continued to flourish in Varanasi. Its high point was the reign of the great Mauryan emperor, Ashoka (272-232 BC). Since his empire covered most of north India, he ruled over what was perhaps the largest and the most powerful state in the world at that

Buddhist monks circumambulating the Dhamek stupa.

But the Buddha left God and divinity out of his system. Being an atheistic religion, Buddhism does not see God as essential to the universe, but acknowledges a natural cosmic rise and decline. It holds that the universe originally had been a place of bliss, but by giving in to desire, man made

Facing page: Image of Buddha in the main temple in Sarnath.
Pages 82-83 overleaf: Devotees gather round the Dhamek stupa wreathed in the early morning mist.

time. Early in his rule, Ashoka fought a bloody battle in Kalinga (now Orissa) for access to its seaports and Chinese trade. Thousands were killed and the country laid waste. Devastated by the carnage, Ashoka renounced violence and adopted the pacifist creed of Buddhism. He used the rest of his long life and the resources of his vast empire to spread the message of Buddhism all over Asia.

At Sarnath there are many monuments

built by the great Ashoka. The Chaukhandi Stupa marks the place where the Buddha preached his first sermon. Ashoka must have undertaken other constructions, but only the first two stupas and a pillar with his inscription survive.

Chaukhandi Stupa: The Chaukhandi Stupa is a simple 98-foot high red brick octagonal structure, situated on a small hillock on the road that goes to Sarnath. A Persian inscription over one of the doorways

believed to be exactly the place where the Buddha preached his second sermon to his first five disciples.

Dharam Rajik Stupa: Only the foundations of the Dharam Rajik Stupa can be seen at Sarnath. This commemorates the preaching of the first sermon by the Buddha in about 519 BC. Originally built by Ashoka, it was levelled down in later ages. Also to be found are the ruins of four monasteries from between the second and fourth centuries AD.

The Bodhi tree under whose branches, Prince Siddhartha gained enlightenment and was known thereafter as the Buddha.

of the stupa states that the octagonal brick tower on top of the building was erected by Gobardhan at the orders of Emperor Akbar in 1589 AD because Akbar's father Humayun once took shelter there!

Dhamek Stupa: The huge Dhamek Stupa marks the place where Buddha preached his first sermon. The Dhamek is an abbreviation of a Sanskrit word *dharmika* which means 'Preacher of Dharma' The site of the stupa is

The Brahmins fought the tide of Buddhism as best as they could but for the next few centuries Buddhism replaced Brahminism as the dominant religion in Varanasi. The Kushan king Kanishka in the first century AD extended state patronage to Buddhism. During the Gupta Age, (from the fourth to the sixth century AD). Sarnath retained its importance and emerged as a major centre of Buddhist art. Exquisite stone statues sculpted during the period are now displayed at the local museum.

According to the Chinese traveller Xuan Zhuang, who came to Varanasi in the seventh century AD, there were 30 monasteries and 3,000 monks in Varanasi. From the eighth century onwards. Hinduism began to regain its former position by virtue of the missionary zeal of the great Hindu preacher Shankaracharya and the active patronage of the Gahadvala kings.

pass. The matter was finally referred to a British officer, and it was then that the British came to know of the existence and importance of Sarnath. An archaeological department was set up and excavations began under the able guidance of Sir John Marshall and Sir Alexander Cunningham. Much of what is on display today in Sarnath was unearthed by these two men.

Mool Gandh Kuti Vihar: Anagrik Dharampal, a Buddhist monk, also played a

Interior of the Thai temple dedicated to Lord Buddha.

Sarnath however continued to flourish till the advent of Islam in the twelfth century. But by the time the British came in the seventeenth century, it had fallen into decay.

At the turn of the century Mahavira Swamy touring the sacred shrines of Buddhism, came to Sarnath and found the place in ruin, with nearby villagers carting away its bricks to build their own houses. The enraged Swamy stood in front of the bullock carts and would not allow them to

major role in the restoration of Sarnath. After much effort he collected enough funds to build the modern Mool Gandh Kuti Vihar in 1939. This is an ancient name for a modern temple built on the spot where the Buddha is said to have rested and meditated during the rains. Today this is the main shrine of Sarnath. It resembles ancient Buddhist monasteries and is made of fine *chunar* (lime) stone. A Japanese artist has painted impressive frescoes on the inside

walls depicting scenes from the life of the Buddha. The main object here is a gold replica of a 5th century Buddha statue now preserved in the Sarnath museum.

A flourishing Bo tree, said to be a direct descendant of the tree in Bodh Gaya under which the Buddha received Enlightenment is planted outside the temple.

Temples representative of Tibetan, Chinese and Burmese Buddhism as well as Jain and Hindu belief are also found in Sarnath. But its mystique is perhaps best exemplified in the Asokan wheel (*chakra*) that modern India adopted as its emblem. The Ashoka Chakra adorns the Indian flag. Its original is in the Sarnath museum, a deeply symbolic link between a young nation and its old past.

Clockwise from above left: Interior of the Japanese temple. Interior of the Tibetan temple. A frontal view of the Tibetan temple. A Korean temple.
Facing page above left, right and below left: Scenes from the Jataka Tales *which tell of incidents from the previous lives of the Buddha.* **Middle:** *The Buddha attaining* parinirvana *or supreme* nirvana, *the final release from the cycle of birth and rebirths. As he lies on his right side, under the sal trees in the suburbs of Kushinagara, he addresses his monks for the last time: 'Brothers, remember these words: everything is perishable. Work out your salvation with diligence.' Then he enters into contemplation and at the end of the last watch, just before dawn, on the first day of the full moon in the month of May, he loses his individuality and becomes universal. The earth shakes, the sal trees blossom and the sky rains down perfumed petals to the sound of divine music.* **Below right:** *The Buddha as soon as he was born, stood up and took seven steps and his footprints turned into lotuses.*

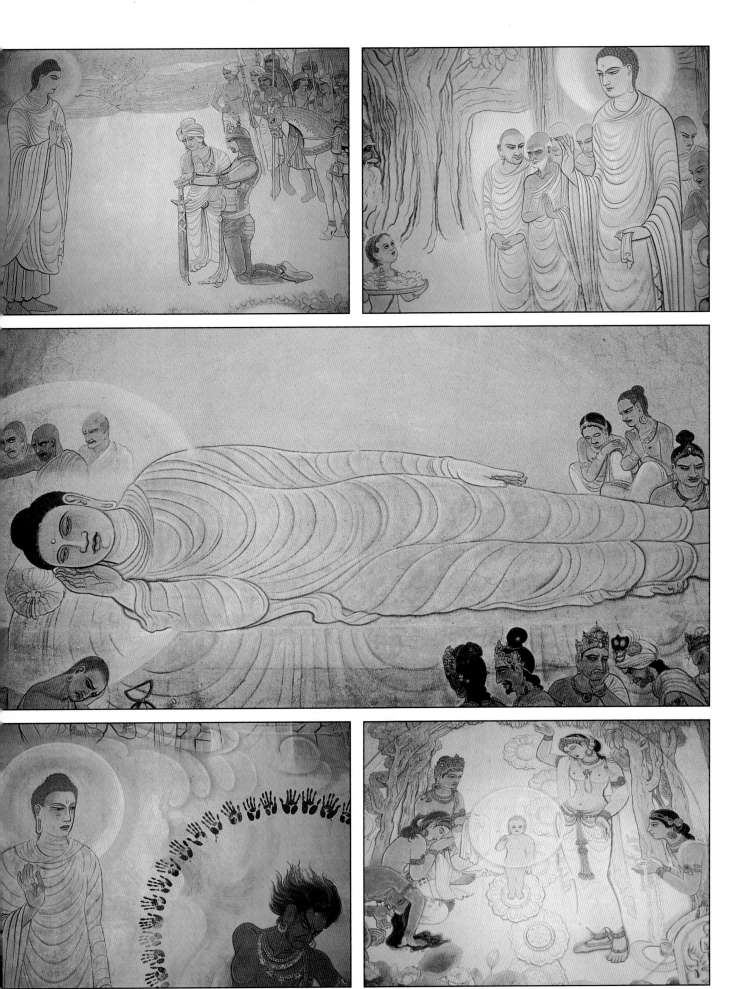

ISBN: 978-81-7436-051-9

© Roli & Janssen BV 2010
Published in India by Roli Books
in arrangement with Roli & Janssen
M-75, Greater Kailash II Market
New Delhi-110 048, India
Phone: ++91-11-4068 2000
Fax: ++91-11-2921 7185
E-mail: info@rolibooks.com
Website: www.rolibooks.com

Photo Credits

Thomas L. Kelly
J.L. Nou
Sanjeev Saith
Dr Chakraverty
Anita Khemka
Pramod Kapoor
Getty Images
Corbis

Fotomedia

Tarun Chopra
Poonam A. Kumar
Dinesh Khanna

Illustrations

A.Z. Ranjeet

Printed and bound at
Star Standard Industries Pte. Ltd., Singapore